POETIC APHORISMS

L'ORIZZONTE
Collana fondata e diretta da
Giovanni Dotoli, Encarnación Medina Arjona, Mario Selvaggio

www.lorizzonte.fr

199

noria.info aga.lorizzonte lharmattan.lorizzonte

GIOVANNI DOTOLI

POETIC APHORISMS

Translated by Eric Turcat

L'Harmattan   aga

Cover art
Tarot card from the Rider-Waite tarot deck,
Illustrated by Pamela Coleman Smith, 1909.
[https://upload.wikimedia.org/wikipedia/commons/
f/ff/RWS_Tarot_21_World.jpg]

© L'Harmattan, 2023
5-7, rue de l'École-Polytechnique
75005 Paris - tél. 0033(1)40467920
http://www.editions-harmattan.fr
ISBN 978-2-14-035059-7

© AGA Arti Grafiche Alberobello, 2023
70011 Alberobello (I - Ba)
Contrada Popoleto, nc - tél. 00390804322044
www.editriceaga.it - info@editriceaga.it
ISBN 978-88-9355-365-0

TRANSLATOR'S PREFACE
Of aphorisms and their lexical mise-en-constellation

Eric Turcat

Oklahoma State University

To my great dismay as a language professional, not to mention my even greater embarrassment as a self-proclaimed etymology aficionado, it took the translation of Giovanni Dotoli's entire book of *Poetic Aphorisms* for me to discover that an aphorism has precious little to do with an amphora. Granted, I was always well aware that, whereas the latter is an artefact originally designed to ferry solids or liquids across the Mediterranean, the former remains a top synonym for a maxim. However, why not imagine, as I clearly did, that an aphorism carries meaning just like an amphora carries wine? To me, an aphorism clearly belonged to the same etymological family as a metaphor or an anaphora. The common stem for all, from an amphora to an aphorism, clearly seemed to be the Greek particle <phor>, abbreviated from the verb *pherein* (to carry). If a metaphor carried meaning beyond (*meta*) its literal interpretation, and an anaphora kept carrying meaning backwards (*ana*) by dint of repetition, then, quite probably, an aphorism would have to be a saying that carried its own meaning either away (*ab*) from common parlance or towards (*ad*) a new form of wisdom. Both probabilities had always made perfect sense to me, and I only needed to verify in which direction etymologists had agreed to take this somewhat strange combination of a Greek stem and a Latin prefix. Of course, as I soon discovered, the answer turned out to be that there was exactly no Greco-Roman combination to be found, and that the etymology of "aphorism" resided squarely in two Greek particles, neither one of which had anything to do with the "carrying" of meaning. So much for my classical education!

An even greater source of dismayed embarrassment came from the realization that, despite writing an entire monograph on La Rochefoucauld's *Maxims*[1], I still had no idea that a "maxim" is only the second definition of an aphorism, at least according to the *Oxford English Dictionary*. The first, although it obviously stresses the notion of concision equally central to a maxim, initially underscores the fundamentally scientific value of the aphorism[2] over the strictly moralistic applications to which I had it ascribed. An aphorism is not the wittiest possible encapsulation of a human code of behavior, it is above all a highly pedagogical tool designed to help learners better memorize key precepts from human sciences such as medicine. More importantly perhaps, and still according to the first sense of the word in the *OED*, an aphorism is essentially a "definition". Hence, as opposed to a maxim, or *maxima sententia*, which quite literally maximizes the rhetorical potential of a sentence destined to be remembered,

---

[1] *La Rochefoucauld par quatre Chemins : les* Maximes *et leurs ambivalences*, Tübingen, Narr, 2013.

[2] "Aphorism: 1. A 'definition' or concise statement of a principle in any science" (https://www.oed.com).

the aphorism takes a resolutely minimalist path in cutting straight to the proverbial chase. Once again, so much for my classical education!

Ironically, of course, it soon came to light that my dual ignorance could hardly have found a better venue. Indeed, I should first state that the main reason for which I chose to translate *Poetic Aphorisms* was not because I had hoped to somehow replicate my aesthetic experience with La Rochefoucauld's *Maxims*. I was not secretly hoping that Dotoli's poetry would mutate into the paradoxical flourishes of Classical French *salon* culture. Quite the contrary, in fact. Because I had previously translated another of the poet's works, and because I also knew Dotoli as a leader in the field of dictionary studies[3], I was already expecting that his *Poetic Aphorisms* would generate the kind of starkness which his verbal equations did immediately deliver. Somewhere, even though I clearly had not yet formulated it in my mind, I must have already expected that aphorisms, all be they as "poetic" as Dotoli's, would indeed resemble scientific definitions far more than the aristocratic quips to which I had become accustomed with maxims.

Furthermore, in finally discovering the etymology of "aphorism" to mean "beyond" (*apo*) the "horizon" (*horismos*), I was instantly reassured that I had made the right

---

[3] Dotoli is the founder and editor of *Cahiers du dictionnaire*, a yearly, scientific publication gathering the proceedings of biannual international conferences, which has been dubbed as *Dictionary Studies* by Classiques Garnier.

decision in bringing *Poetic Aphorisms* to none other than L'Harmattan's "L'Orizzonte" collection. Not only, was I broadening my own horizons, quite literally, by discovering the unexpected meaning of a word that I mistakenly thought I knew, but in so doing, and with greater serendipity yet, I was also furthering the stated mission of a book series that prides itself precisely on offering the broadest possible array of aesthetic perspectives[4]. In moving beyond the horizon of my own ignorance, I was quite simply delving into the core of what the best of aphoristic discourses should and, in this case, do provide, namely a meta-semiosis, or a reflection on the meaning of meaning.

To put it more precisely, if an aphorism is originally a definition, then a "poetic" aphorism is, by extension, the creation of a definition beyond the original definition, or a meta-definition. The poet does not simply create meaning out of a vacuum, but out of a set of lexically predetermined meanings which must then be recreated along the line of a perpetually shifting horizon. Despite its apparent singularity, nothing seems more plural than a poetic horizon, especially when the poetry defines itself as a plurality of aphorisms, or, etymologically speaking, as horizons beyond the horizon. In linguistic terms, it could therefore be argued that an aphorism, just like a horizon - or a defi-

---

[4] From L'Harmattan's webpage: « L'Orizzonte est une collection multidisciplinaire et multilingue des sciences humaines, dans l'unité de la « culture » et d'une panoplie de nouvelles perspectives. »

nition for that matter - is not simply a noun but a deixis[5]. Its meaning continually shifts as the reference point of the observer changes. Just like a dictionary definition may invite the cross-referencing of several other definitions before the entirety of a semantic field becomes apparent, the poet's aphorisms must also cross-reference with one another in order to paint a fuller picture of what one could call the artist's world view.

Nobel laureate André Gide, might have chosen to subsume this constant, deictic shift of poetic meaning into the critical metaphor of his famous *mise-en-abyme*[6]. And why not? Is there not a depth effect to the apparent superficiality of aphorisms? Does the horizon of poetic creation not remain even when the poet has taken strides towards attaining his own creative objectives? On both counts, the affirmative could hardly jump into sharper re-

---

[5] Defined as the linguistic function of "pointing out" (https://www. oed.com), the term "deixis" was initially coined by German Neogrammarians, Hermann Osthoff and Karl Bruggman, in their six-volume survey of what would later be known as Indo-European languages: *Morphologische Untersuchungen auf dem Gebiete der indogermanischen Sprachen* (1878-1910). More recent linguistic terminology has also referred to deixes as "shifters" (Roman Jakobson, *Essais de linguistique générale*, tome 1, Paris, Minuit, 1963, chap. 9).

[6] Gide, himself, borrowed the expression from medieval heraldry where the *abyme* represented the inescutcheon of a coat of arms, or the shield within the shield: « J'aime assez qu'en une œuvre d'art on retrouve ainsi transposé, à l'échelle des personnages, le sujet même de cette œuvre par comparaison avec ce procédé du blason qui consiste, dans le premier, à mettre le second en abyme » (André Gide, *Journal*, tome 1 (1887-1925), Paris, Gallimard, « Pléiade », 1996, p. 149).

lief. More remarkably yet, and partially because of its maverick misspelling of *abîme*, Gide's *mise-en-abyme* also indicates that the depth effect of certain types of artistic pursuit extends well beyond horizontal perception and into the depths of a seemingly bottomless "abyss". Hence, more specifically, the poetic horizon of aphorisms does not simply keep reaching horizontally into the singular depth of its creator's field of vision but also vertically into the plural depths of a fully three-dimensional mindscape.

However, where the Gidian analogy fails to illuminate the full scope of Dotolian poetry is in its romantic (some might even say pre-Sartrean) fascination with the downward gaze. Contrary to Gide, Dotoli has little time for the Nietzschean musings of Natanaël's interlocutor or for the amoral dilettantism of Lafcadio's *acte gratuit*[7]. When the author of *Poetic Aphorisms* exercises his vertical gaze, he does not stare down into the abyss of antisocial egoism, but he looks upward into the heavens, where the only darkness to be seen is the one disappearing in starlight. Indeed, as I had somewhat coincidentally observed in the closing words to both the preface of my previous translation[8] and a review of Dotoli's *Liberté et droits de*

---

[7] Let us recall how Gide's two most Nietzschean lessons stem first from *Les nourritures terrestres* (Paris, Mercure de France, 1897), where Ménalque delivers his infamous, family-phobic message to young Natanël ("Familles ! Je vous hais !", p. 83), and second, from *Les caves du Vatican* (Paris, Gallimard, 1914) where Lafcadio spirals into the homicidal urge to throw a perfect stranger from a train, just because he can do so gratuitously (p. 485).

l'homme[9], as grounded as the poet's perspective might prove, his gaze invariably shifts back to the vertical as his contemplations return almost obsessively skywards to the stars.

What has struck me here, throughout the translation of *Poetic Aphorisms*, has been what I now consider far less of a coincidence and far more of a clearly structured semantic pattern. Whereas stars continue to abound in this particular collection of poems as much as they do in much of Dotoli's poetry, this time, it is their clusters that capture the imagination, and right from the outset, since the poet himself shares this query at the very start of his introduction: "Did our Being speak in fragments, word after word, sound after sound, sign after sign, like a poem of stars in a scattered constellation?[10]" If, by virtue of its lexical choices, an aphorism were to be read as a constellation where each star symbolized a word, and if, due to its cumulative structure, each poetic cluster of aphorisms were to be interpreted as a constellation of constellations, would it not then follow that the book itself could be approached as a constellation of meta-constellations? What if *Poetic Aphorisms* actually could be read not just in frag-

[8] "Treacherous Translators and Other Straw Man Fallacies." *Chance Freedom,* tr. E. Turcat & H. Farris, Paris, L'Harmattan, 2023, p. 7-19.

[9] "Les pieds sur terre et la tête dans les étoiles : l'Impossible possible de *Liberté et droits de l'homme." Noria. Revue littéraire et artistique* 5 (2023), p. 19-35.

[10] *Infra*, p. 29.

ments but as a semantic web of lexical clusters? How might one begin to draw this web? How would one then proceed to recognize those clusters? And how should one finally interpret the book as a whole in light of its brightest constellations? As all these questions came to mind, it seemed clear that Dotoli's aphorisms would soon be rising far beyond their etymological horizon, and far higher than even Gide's decidedly three-dimensional *mise-en-abyme*. What I now needed was a clear method to diagram, analyze, then synthesize what I was beginning to perceive as an overarching *mise-en-constellation*.

Unsurprisingly for one trained in the reassuringly binary ways of structuralism, my prosaic mind immediately gravitated to numbers. Dotoli's poetry, as I recalled, was definitely one that I had come to associate with numerology[11], so my first order of business would be to simply count how many poems, or aphoristic clusters, had been gathered in composing the final version of the book. The answer was twenty-two. And right away I had struck gold! Indeed, for those of us less familiar with astrology, it should be noted that twenty-two is precisely the number of Major Arcana in a deck of tarot cards. Furthermore, the only direct definition of the word "star" given by Dotoli is to be found in "Flowers", the eighteenth poem of his book: "Star = flower of the sky". Given that the Major Arcana are num-

---

[11] "My date of birth is 6 6 6 / 4 + 2 is also 6 and 9 is 3 3 3 / A beautiful numerological coincidence / To be delivered into the world on that very day" (G. Dotoli, *Chance Freedom*, *op. cit.*, p. 61).

bered zero through twenty-one, and that the eighteenth poem therefore corresponds to the seventeenth Arcanum, it turns out that, in tarot, Arcanum seventeen is also called "The Star". Without necessarily attempting to do so on a conscious level, Dotoli had managed to align his "star" with that of the larger, astrological framework. All that remained for me to do at that point was to align his poems in such a way as to expose any further dialogue, this time between the poems themselves. To that end, I would need to work with two decks, one vertically and the other horizontally, and I would have to count the number of instances in which one card/word/poem title resonated with each of the other twenty-one. This would help me define the densest lexical clusters, which, in turn, would allow me to reach at least some conclusions regarding Dotoli's otherwise elusive pursuit of meaning.

Here is what my structuralist "tarot" table yielded[12]:

---

[12] Five of the poem titles/key words have been abbreviated as follows: <Lang.> for "Language"; <Literat.> for "Literature"; <Enthus.> for "Enthusiasm"; <Intuit.> for "Intuition"; and <Convers> for "Conversation". As indicated by the presence of totals at the bottom of each of its two pages, the table should be read in columns, not rows. The first total tallies the *mise-en-constellation*, or the number of times a particular key word appears in each poem, but not the number of occurrences of the word itself within its own, eponymous poem (hence the X markers that appear across the table, in a diagonal). The second total, inside parentheses, computes what the number would have been if all occurrences of the key word had been taken into consideration, not just counting the uses from the matching, titular poem, but also from Dotoli's introduction ("Enter").

	Being	Art	Lang.	Music	Artist
Being	X	0	0	0	0
Art	1	X	1	1	1
Lang.	0	0	X	0	0
Music	2	0	0	X	0
Artist	2	0	0	0	X
Poetry	1	1	3	1	0
Heart	0	0	1	1	0
Literat.	0	0	2	0	0
Enthus.	3	0	1	0	0
Intuit.	1	1	2	0	0
Love	0	0	0	0	0
Convers.	0	0	3	0	0
Pleasure	1	1	0	0	0
Truth	0	0	0	0	0
Beauty	1	2	0	0	0
Time	0	0	0	0	0
Color	0	1	1	1	0
Flowers	0	0	0	1	0
Other	1	0	2	1	0
Science	0	0	0	0	0
Light	0	0	0	0	0
Life	1	0	0	0	0
Totals	14 (50)	6 (56)	16 (37)	6 (33)	1 (36)

Poetry	Heart	Literat.	Enthus.	Intuit.	Love
1	3	0	0	0	0
0	2	0	0	0	0
1	0	0	0	0	1
1	2	0	0	0	0
0	3	0	0	0	1
X	2	0	0	0	2
2	X	0	0	0	1
0	0	X	0	0	1
1	1	0	X	0	0
0	0	0	0	X	0
0	6	0	1	0	X
1	0	0	0	0	1
0	0	0	0	0	3
0	1	0	0	0	0
1	2	0	0	0	0
1	1	0	0	0	2
1	1	0	0	0	1
0	0	0	0	0	0
0	1	0	0	0	4
3	1	0	0	0	3
0	1	0	0	0	1
4	1	0	0	0	4
17 (70	28 (67)	0 (40)	1 (39)	0 (41)	25 (85)

	Convers.	Pleasure	Truth	Beauty	Time
Being	0	0	0	0	0
Art	0	0	0	1	0
Lang.	0	0	0	0	0
Music	0	0	0	0	0
Artist	0	0	0	1	2
Poetry	0	0	0	0	0
Heart	0	0	0	0	1
Literat.	0	0	1	0	0
Enthus.	0	0	0	0	1
Intuit.	0	0	0	0	0
Love	0	0	0	1	1
Convers.	X	0	0	0	1
Pleasure	0	X	0	0	1
Truth	0	0	X	0	0
Beauty	0	1	2	X	0
Time	0	1	0	0	X
Color	0	0	0	2	1
Flowers	0	0	1	2	2
Other	0	0	0	0	0
Science	0	0	0	0	0
Light	0	0	0	0	2
Life	0	1	0	0	5
Totals	0 (37)	3 (37)	4 (35)	7 (43)	17 (57)

Color	Flowers	Other	Science	Light	Life
0	0	0	0	1	2
1	0	0	0	1	2
0	0	0	0	0	1
0	0	0	0	0	0
0	0	0	0	1	0
0	0	0	0	0	2
0	0	0	0	0	2
0	0	0	0	1	1
0	0	0	0	1	2
0	0	0	0	1	0
0	0	3	0	3	1
0	0	0	0	2	0
0	0	0	0	0	1
0	0	0	0	0	1
0	0	0	0	0	1
0	0	0	0	0	5
X	0	0	0	3	8
0	X	0	0	0	2
0	0	X	0	2	3
2	0	0	X	1	1
1	0	0	0	X	0
1	0	0	0	1	X
5 (43)	0 (34)	3 (51)	0 (43)	18 (79)	35 (96)

In terms of which word resonates the most with the twenty-one others in Dotoli's purposely minimalist lexicon, the result comes as no surprise. Just like the title of the final poem, "Life", scores a 96 in terms of its lexical frequency throughout the book, its score is also the highest in terms of constellating with all the other titles (35). The second highest *mise-en-constellation*, however, does not fully correlate with the numbers for lexical frequency. Whereas "Love" and "Poetry" respectively take the second and third position as far as how many times they are repeated throughout the entire work (85 and 70 respectively), only "Love" persists in the top three for lexical cross-referencing between the poems, with a count of 25. In second position, with a 26-count, comes the word "Heart" that apparently constellates better than "Poetry", which only claims fifth place in terms of cross-referencing outside its eponymous poem (17). Therefore, the prime structural surprise of *Poetic Aphorisms* comes from the paradox that, despite its third-place ranking overall (70), "Poetry" itself does not correlate as strongly with the other twenty-one poems as the less expected "Heart" whose tally of 67 was initially keeping it down in fifth place overall.

In fact, if instead of simply absorbing the intensity of a *mise-en-constellation*, based on the sheer quantity of its cross-referencing across the table, one were to further count the number of key words with which each poem title interacts, one would also realize that "Heart" now ties with "Life" for first place. Both words resonate with no fewer than fifteen other titles in the book, which puts them both ahead of "Love" (13 interactions) and even farther ahead of "Poetry", which, once again drops to fifth place with 11 resonances. To say that *Poetic Aphorisms*, based upon their dictionary-like structure, convey a strictly *ars gratia artis* impression, would not only be an oversight, it would quite simply be a mistake. In spite of its deeply cerebral nature, Dotoli's poetry still appears to place less of a premium on the modernism of his otherwise Mallarmean model[13], and more on fine-tuning the strings of his heart's lyre.

Back to the intensity of the meaning generated by a particular word constellation, the one title pairing that immediately catches the eye, with eight overlaps inside just one poem, is the "Life" - "Color" duo. Clearly, Dotoli intends his colorful imagination to vibrate with life. Yet, surprisingly, the reverse cannot be verified, since the poem "Color" only comprises one lexical reference to "Life". In this particular case, the light does not shine both ways, and the constellation turns out to be more of an optical illusion. However, a closer look at the table then reveals a far more reciprocating constellation in the "Life" – "Time" pair. Indeed, whether in the former poem or in the latter, both titles refer to the other's key word exactly five times within their respective texts. Of

---

[13] Consider, for instance, Dotoli's repeated paratextual references to "Un coup de dés jamais n'abolira le hasard" in *Chance Freedom* (*op. cit.* p. 23 et 90).

course, this particular *mise-en-constellation* could hardly be any more appropriate, given *Poetic Aphorisms'* general dismissal of the navel-gazing, angst-ridden obsession with death so characteristic of romantic literature. As we are once again reminded on the most macro-structural level, Dotoli's poetry takes a far more Bergsonian view of time as a life-affirming force far brighter than any pendulum-ticking, raven-fearing, spectral morbidity à la Edgar Allen Poe. Because if "Life is the labyrinth of time", it is also true that "Time = Life's pleasure", and therefore that no Thanatos may be derived from navigating the labyrinthine Eros of artistic creation.

In sum, it would appear that, through its constant *mise-en-constellation* of titles, Dotoli's repertoire of *Poetic Aphorisms* selects at least three cards for the tarot reading of its lexical cross-referencing. The first, and least surprising, given the sheer quantity of its iterations throughout the book, confirms the celebration of "Life" over any form of self-pitying, narcissistic death-drive. The second, and least expected, due to its structural emergence as an equally vital lexical presence from one chapter to the next, reveals a "Heart" that never falters on the path of anguish or pathology but that energizes the poetic process both through its courage and its generosity[14]. The third, and certainly the most punctual in its ability to constellate on

---

[14] "The heart toils / The heart breathes out the word / The heart gives [...] At night the heart rests / So that life's struggles may begin anew / Each morning" (p. 54).

par with "Life" itself, affirms the fundamentally human value of "Time", not as a source of existential crisis, but as an essence of core creativity[15].

For the final hermeneutic twist, however, let us turn back to this three card/word/title *mise-en-constellation* on our structuralist 'tarot' table. Beyond their etymological horizon, and now beyond the semantic interpretation of the "Life" – "Heart" – "Time" cluster as an Eros of courage defined by duration, what could this very elementary three-card pull also signify at the most basic, astrological level? One last time, let us consider the numbers of the three cards selected from the twenty-two-card deck of Major Arcana. First comes "Life" at number twenty-one, also known as "The World" card; second, "Heart" at number six, otherwise referred to as "The Lovers"; and third, "Time" at number fifteen, best remembered as "The Devil". If the first card gives a reading of the poet's mind, then "change of place" originally defines the nature of his musings[16], which hardly comes as a surprise since the most noticeable absentee in the *Poetic Aphorisms* of our interstellar, time traveler is precisely that of traveling. But if the second card provides insight into the artist's body of work, then "trials overcome" suddenly appear as defining

[15] "Time is not an abyss = it is the locus of poetry" (p. 81).

[16] According to Arthur Edward Waite, poet, scholar and mystic: "21. THE WORLD. - Assured success, recompense, voyage, route, emigration, flight, change of place" (*The Pictorial Key to the Tarot*, London, Rider & Son, 1911). https://en.wikisource.org/wiki/The_Pictorial_Key_to_the_Tarot

factors[17], which, given Dotoli's consistently productive poetic career over the past two decades, could hardly provide more of a revelation. And if the third card speaks to the soul of the artist's creative being, then "extraordinary efforts" further dispel the myth of a seemingly Saturnian artistic process[18]. Behind the serenity of the Apollonian aphorist always lurks the Dionysian daemon of poetry... As if the star-crossing poet himself could ever conceal the devilishly cunning origins of his art: "My date of birth is 6 6 6"!

---

[17] Still according to Waite: "6. THE LOVERS. —Attraction, love, beauty, trials overcome. Reversed: Failure, foolish designs. Another account speaks of marriage frustrated and contrarieties of all kinds" (*ibid.*).

[18] Waite again: "15. THE DEVIL. —Ravage, violence, vehemence, extraordinary efforts, force, fatality; that which is predestined but is not for this reason evil. Reversed: Evil fatality, weakness, pettiness, blindness" (*ibid.*).

POETIC APHORISMS

ENTER

Was speech an aphorism in its very formative beginnings?

Did our Being speak in fragments, word after word, sound after sound, sign after sign, like a poem of stars in a scattered constellation?

It must have lasted for ages.

Was speech a sort of abbreviated saying? A short and proverbial style?

I think so.

It was poetic from the moment it appeared, giving shape to the world.

Over time, it was led by experience towards less syntagmatic, more organized structures.

In his Treatise on Style, Louis Aragon asserts that "Humanity loves speaking in proverbs".

By this he means: poetically, through fulgurations of languages.

It is popular wisdom. Ancestral words continually mouthed through our Being.

Brevity is a poetic act.

Aphorisms are its sublime translation.

Man's voice proceeds in fragments. It cannot be linear. It is fragmentary. Images come in succession, as on film, through double exposure. And the text is collated, through successive fulgurations.

Does Montaigne not write: "All of us are a patchwork made from such diverse and shapeless contexture that each piece, each moment, plays its own game" (Essays II, 1, "Of the Inconstancy of Our Actions")?

Texts - mostly poems - are a dissemination. Their composition cannot be regular. Down with straight lines. Their appearance is sinuous, fragmented, disorganized. The author's voice is ruled by fragmentary variation.

What is the rhythm of a poem? It will be a matter of asystematic lines, searching for balance, comparing knowledge for its refinement. And nonetheless, the book will of course be one, as all poems, from the longest to the shortest. Fantasies and imaginations follow in close succession like beads on a heart-strung rosary.

Here is the proof that no truth is ever definitive, and that fragmentary rhythm signifies the texture of language. In a general framework, the poet inserts his stars, his word grafts, to explain the human condition.

The poem is a corpus that tells the tale of life. Its words are plots that stamp the synthesis of writing. Provisional configurations signal the edgy mobility of language. The text is restless like the voice. It is a polyphonic web that proceeds through commentary and continual interpretations.

It is a game between light and darkness. The evidence is mysterious and enigmatic. Shadows conceal the evidence.

Lines are layered usage. They are a kneading that spreads a "seed" (Montaigne, Essays I, 40, "A Consideration on Cicero"). That is why they carry a sense of quotation, polyphonic rhythm and concatenated speech.

Graft upon graft, the text proceeds infinitely, in a rewriting of words and their rhythm.

Words are transitioning, from one point to another. They circulate as instants, humors, annotations, fragments of orality and writing. Everything is provisional, spontaneous, experimental, gestational.

A network of words proceeds on the rails deep within the soul, making light of bookish knowledge and accumulated culture. From fragment to fragment and analysis to analysis, the book makes its own way, travels, extends its motions, through accords and discords.

Each aphorism speaks of the instant in transition. Again, I rely on Montaigne: "Words retold take on different sounds and different meanings" (Essays III, 1, "Of use value and honesty"). Meaning is immediate, seasonal, ephemeral, temporary, fleeting.

Does duration exist? The poem searches through the instantaneity of words, the patchwork of utterances, the beads of language, which are illusions of continuity. Aphorisms tell of instability and "fumbling in the dark" (Montaigne, Essays, I, 25, "Of the education of children").

The text wanders through repetitions and instantaneous voices. It floats on the rhythm of repetition, the carpe diem of harmony, the psychological time of our soul.

Is this not a form of victory over death, as in an average movie? We reach the climax of our being through the swaying of our words, teetering and profound, repeated and present.

The poem is a plurality of instants, of winds coming and going, of paradoxical tautologies, as precarious and suspensive as life.

The voice of instantaneity is that of Rimbaud's "real life". The text is a concatenation of instants going back and forth, of experiences, of medleys, of words flowing like the wind. It is fluid, gestural and unstable, for it conveys the appearance of speech.

My Poetic aphorisms are a spoken book.

They recount words and their poetic motives, bordering on simplicity, which is a sign of profundity.

Being

$\mathcal{I}$ write therefore I am

One day my Being will be a star

Light comes from Being

Conscience of Being = the way of the journey

Sole goal of Being = aspiring to the heavens

The earth is round = I am its being

One must always be oneself = Being

Being is living

The comedy of the world is the comedy of Being

Leaving is letting breathe your Being

Ontology of Being = journey of life

Celebration = that of Being

God is the minister of Being

Rich heart = explosion of Being

Man defines the course of his Being

Woman = ideal of Being

Child = surprise of Being

Little girl = poetry of Being

Man + point + star = journey of Being

Looking out the window
= discovering the infinity of Being

Soul = companion of Being

To dream one must live in Being

To succeed one must be a poet

Well-being is a tremor of the heart

My ideal = the voice of silence
= therefore Being avant-garde

A waltz note = the heart spins its Being

Blonde + brunette + redhead
= sun + heavenly Being

Compliments = the eye of Being

Innocent gaze = vision of Being

My star = the road to Being

Purity + lightning = to live your Being well in advance

Dazzling fervor of Being

Charming face = the life of Being resumes

I am a Being

I behave as a Poet-Being

Being = Union of Beings

Art

School is out
Art is us

Emotion?
Rather a cry for art

Art = a different gaze

A blade of grass holds the secret of art

A bird takes flight = the heart follows it = art flies

Geometric lines = dream crossings = this is the art of life

A painter reads the depths of art

A sculptor measures the height of art

An architect stays at the edge of art

The artist is never individual
His art is democratic

Art = universal language

Art or autobiography

Art = total confidence

A portrait is never a stroke of art

Art sees

Art invents

Art hates vulgarity

Art is life

Art is a rose

Art = new horizons

Art = here

Art or the rose of a spot

Art is told by the stars

Art is a blue rainbow

Art is an incurable fever

Art is never an illusion

Light concentrates on art

Taste of art = taste of eternity

The heart's rhythm is the sheet music of art

Art leads to the moon

The moon watches art

Art or the energy of living

Art is an unexpected movement

Art gives transparency to things

When I see towers linked by a rope
I tell myself = this is art

Through art I look inwards

Stone keeps the secret of art
Art will illuminate it

Art paints dreams in color

Workshop of the universe = workshop of art

Art knows the lines of the unknown

Art has a brother
Bird
Between sea and sky

Art creates beauty

Art = knowledge of Being

Art = path of destiny for humanity

Art survives everything

Art transforms the world

Art recreates

Language

Language = word of God

Language = love of words

Orchestrating words = orchestrating language

The moon speaks the language of purity

Procession of stars = procession of language

Language gives voice to the hearth

A star = a language
Respect it

No artifice in language

Memory finds itself in language

Blue thread is the transparency of language

Mother tongue = that of infinity

I come from an original

The words of language come directly from Paradise

I speak = I am a linguist of language

My signs are the original alphabet of language

The cosmos has its language = that of man

Grass has a language = that of poetry

Where is my poem? = in the language of life

The gaze is a rhythm
Lines of a language

Experience is a language

Babel?
No separation
Of the union of languages
In language

Music

$\mathcal{D}$ancing heart = musical Being

On the edge of the brook
Listen to the water's music

Musical line = rhythm of bygone days

Dreams speak their music to me

Seven musical notes
At the crossroads of the world = the mystery is revealed

To begin the dream
A few symphonic notes

Stone keeps the most ancient music

Trees play aerial music

Leaves are musical notes

On the seventh day
God discovered
The high pitch of musical notes

Sand sings the music of silence

Water plays accordion music

The cherry tree launches a music as sweet as your lips

Childhood is music in A major

The flight of a butterfly
Towards the music of a star

Music is a quest

Music is the hinterland

Feverish ideal = pointed music

Music cancels the void

No more brambles on a journey
Illuminated by music

The horizon is a musical

Clarity of signs = illumination of music

I live in the Church of Music

Music or poetry?
Both

Only one diamond = musical notes

My ego shows
In the sheet music of the heart = music of Being

The artist

The artist unites creation

The artist transforms chaos into harmony

The artist captures the original meaning

Through the window of the world
The artist reads the stars

The artist connects all the threads of the universe

The artist plows mysteries

The artist watches over the heart's path

The artist has but one place = the heart of Being

The stone is the artist's locker

The artist tells the timely and untimely

The artist = warning

The artist is he who knows

The artist sends but one reminder = that of existence

The artist is the accountant of transparency

The artist sees the light on the road

The artist alone discovers the meaning of myth

The artist has but one weapon = that of his mind

The artist's field is that of doubt

The artist and the sea have the same eye

The artist swims in the original water

The artist = a wide-eyed dreamer

One being for infinity = the artist

The artist never sleeps

The artist is starved for purity

The artist is the sleeper of Eternity

The artist is the prince of freedom

The artist interprets the harmony of things

The motherland of the artist is the world

The artist follows the path of his illusion

The artist does keep up with fashion

The artist is a creator of shapes

The artist = he who makes the heart speak

The artist = psychiatric doctor of the world

The artist = he who loves beauty

Poetry

Poetry affirms

Poetry knows

Poetry translates

Poetry = music

Poetry reveals

Poetry comes to life

Poetry cannot be defined

Poetry = fulguration

Poetry = unity

Poetry is at the heart of the One

Poetry lives eternally

Poetry is a rose

Poetry and a rose
Only one path

Poetry is breath

Poetry is astonishment

Poetry goes straight to the heart of secrets

Poetry = the inconceivably conceivable

Poetry perceives

Poetry reads

Poetry transfigures

Poetry = magic

Poetry = anti-language

Poetry is a sign

Of what does poetry speak
Of grass of the moon of trees of the heavens
And of love

Poetry strums a gold thread

Poetry = the only possible path

Poetry is fragile
And strong as the ancestral stone

Poetry sets fire to the last ashes

Poetry is the soul's fire

Poetry = sign

Poetry listens to the wind's voice

Poetry is the quest for meaning

Poetry transforms nothingness into a star

Poetry scintillates in praesentia

Poetry = total energy

Poetry = mud turned into gold

Poetry is naked
And heavenly dressed

Poetry never rambles

Poetry = the eternal modernity of life

Poetry = the art of synthesis

Poetry = cartography of existence

Poetry = religion without God as a landmark

Poetry is not an illness

Poetry = the language of the soul

Poetry is essential

Poetry = an enigmatic narration of the world that surrounds us

Poetry = the language of love

Poetry = the liberation of Being

Poetry = an eye on the invisible

Poetry = the search for lost snow

Poetry is the sound of my red accordion

Poetry = an opening to the freedom of illusion

The heart

The heart lives in poetry

The heart keeps the secret of meaning

The heart signifies

The heart is the locus of experience

The heart is the library of poetry

The heart plays any musical score

The heart knows words

The heart does not beat
It bursts into rhythm

The heart is not romantic
It is a crystallization

The heart is the cornerstone of time

The heart is the locus of formulation

The heart is not the place of emotion
It is the place of creation

The heart toils

The heart breathes out the word

The heart gives

The heart recounts the moment

The heart does not expose
It formulates

The heart is dawn

The heart contemplates

The heart gives rhythm to origins

The heart speaks the mind

The heart is never empty

The heart governs the body and the mind

Heart = dynamism

Heart = life's lantern

Every morning the heart exclaims
Oh!!!

The heart is a cry

The heart is a transfer

The heart is the arch of language

The heart talks to itself

The heart is the seat of freedom

Man is always searching for a heart

The heart is as impenetrable as the ocean

At night the heart rests
So that life's struggles may begin anew
Each morning

The heart defies the stars

The heart is the mysterious locus of love

Literature

Literature is everything

Language is nothing without literature

Literature + language = an indivisible binomial

Literature has the right to speak

I fight against small-time literature

Literature knows

Literature abhors cliché

Literature invents

Literature is novelty

Literature is travel

Literature is the way

Literature breathes fire

Literature sings words

Literature is a surprise

Literature believes

Literature is never at a deficit

Literature is a magnetic field

Literature never doubts itself

Literature combines the truth

Literature has but one formula = that of its own energy

Literature = vision

Literature knows the world's harmony

Literature lives in the light

Literature speaks

Literature is not a system
It is magma

Literature deciphers

Literature tells of Wholeness and Unity

Literature lives in lightning

Literature lives in the world

Literature = reality

Literature is value

Literature = memory of the world

Literature is the world upside down

Literature hardly feeds your man

Literature tells of the century's ailment

Literature is lived life

Literature loves the poverty of essence

Literature is spoken consciousness

Literature is the ear of silence

Enthusiasm

Enthusiasm is life's real law

The sun is a symbol of enthusiasm

The identity of being is enthusiasm

Enthusiasm is the fire of poetry

The heart sees through the lantern of enthusiasm

Enthusiasm = divine fire

Enthusiasm knows no narcissism

Enthusiasm is the seal of language

Passion is found in enthusiasm

Passion = the law of happiness

Joy of being = enthusiasm

Enthusiasm is not a trade

Enthusiasm sings

Enthusiasm is lightning

Enthusiasm has no patronage

Enthusiasm is the shiver of life

Enthusiasm plays with mystery

Enthusiasm = commitment

Enthusiasm does not suffocate

Enthusiasm is a breath of air

Enthusiasm is the oxygen of speech

Enthusiasm has a master key

Enthusiasm = a vocation

Enthusiasm = a thunder of light

Enthusiasm is the innocence of freedom

Enthusiasm marries responsibility

Enthusiasm is cosmic energy

Enthusiasm is the paradigm of time

Enthusiasm is grace

Enthusiasm reveals

Enthusiasm does not conceal

Enthusiasm is God's conduct

Enthusiasm pervades obscurity

Enthusiasm leads to clairvoyance

Enthusiasm = Being in trance

Enthusiasm is God within

Enthusiasm = ardor + fervor + passion + zeal + enthusiasm + joy + frenzy = the poet in action

Intuition

Intuition = the presence of memory

Intuition is the thunderbolt of creation

Intuition is the mind's secret energy

Intuition = simultaneous reality

Intuition = fulgurating vision

Intuition = immediate writing

Intuition = acting without borders

I write to the rhythm of my intuition

Intuition = dizzying imagination

Intuition never thinks

Intuition does not wait

Intuition is as light as the wind

Intuition is the language of Being

Intuition = fulguration

Intuition = the world's epic poem

Intuition = lyricism of lightning

Intuition = narrating without narrative

Intuition does not qualify

Intuition = translation = light = universal gathering

Intuition = dialogue between peoples

Intuition = blitz-painting

Intuition is not consciousness

Intuition is plural

Intuition is not an ism

Intuition is the seven arts improvising

Intuition does not proceed in genres

Intuition is the visionary ego

My accordion practices intuition
= driven by the energy of my fingers

Intuition = pointed synthesis

Intuition creates

Intuition dazzles me

Intuition is a poetic act

Intuition goes beyond space

Intuition burns everything

Intuition has only one language

Intuition paints the moment

Intuition is multidisciplinary

Intuition is a spark

My style? = that of intuition

Intuition invents

Love

Love unites the cosmos

Love is the sign of fraternity

Love is the moon's fire

Love = illumination

Love is the world's gaze

Love acts in the labyrinth of time

Love is anti-nothingness

Love = nudity

Love = the heart's elegy

Love is the finest correspondence

Snow on the world = universal love

Tears of love set the heart on fire

Love is jasmine in the garden

Love knows no twilight

Love drives the wings of birds and humans

Love is the world's dawn

Love opens hearts

Love is the dove of peace

Love = a light

Love is a sublime virtue

Love is wheat

Love is wind

Man's salvation is love

Love is a process of initiation

Love = the body's dew

Love reveals the absolute

Love is a river of lights

Love = pain + enthusiasm

Love = infinite flame

Loves leads to the garden of childhood

Love is the dove's snow

Love is a cry in the night

Love is the astral scout

Love = sweet tyranny

Love cannot be contained

Love = anti-prudence

Love = anti-reflection

Love is all

Without love one does not live

The field of love is as vast as the heavens

Love is a spotlight

How many loves are there?
Maybe five = for the world the other God beauty day in
day out

Love travels from its own heart
To the heart of the other

Love = abnegation

Love = loss of self

Love = innovation continues

Love = heaven within everyone's reach

Love = antilogical

Love = total life

Love = impatience for the other

Love = moving soul

Love = je ne sais quoi of passion

Love = anti-bohemian

My dream = to live in love

Love = adoration + piety + altruism + devotion + eroti-
cism + sex + madness

Love is not sorrow

Love is the heart-body's deed

Conversation

Conversation = word's revelation

Conversation is a love song

Conversation is creative

Conversation invigorates speech

Conversation lives in the imagination

Conversation is spoken writing

Conversation is a crystal

Conversation is balance

Conversation = mediation

Conversation gives language a horizon

Conversation is a light in the darkness

Conversation = light of language

Conversation innervates speech

Conversation is the poetry of the moment

Conversation writes movement

Conversation is an anti-abyss

Conversation is a cavalcade of words

Conversation is a filament of words

Conversation is an olive leaf

Conversation inhabits language

Conversation carries

Conversation breathes

Conversation will not let go

Conversation is the welding of time

Conversation assembles presence

Conversation is identity

Conversation flows like water

Conversation is a breath of wind

Conversation is the rhythm of foliage

Conversation is the ember of friendship

Conversation is the fulguration of destiny

Conversation is one-on-one

Conversation = continuous resuscitation

Conversation = communication

Conversation does not like platitudes

Conversation = commerce + company + intimacy
+ speech + fragments + allusions + rhythm

Pleasure

Pleasure pleases

Pleasure is an art

Pleasure is a path to love

Touching is loving for pleasure

The right word is a sign of pleasure

Pleasure = imagination

Wild pleasure always follows pain

True pleasure grabs you by the gut

Every being is entitled to pleasure

Giving pleasure is more beautiful than receiving it

Pleasure is never crass

Pleasure is a sublime taste

Pleasure is the euphoria of love

Pleasure = happiness + senses + gaze + libido + satisfac-
tion + flight + journey

Pleasure = pursuit of happiness

Pleasure charms

Pleasure thrills

Pleasure delights

Pleasure = anywhere

Pleasure = enjoyment

Pleasure = emotion

Pleasure = love = intensity of time

Pleasure = looking = finding

Pleasure = rejoicing

Pleasure = a full life

Pleasure = anti-sorrow + anti-pain + anti-ennui

Pleasure = positive anxiety

Pleasure = optimism

Pleasure = thunderbolt of poetic memory

Pleasure = burn-free

Pleasure is like silence = it begins with vertigo

Pleasure is a form of salvation

Pleasure is rain inside the body

Truth

Truth is relative

Truth is not always favorable

One must never hurt the truth

Truth is sometimes too true

Between truth and happiness there is a strong bond

Should all truths be known?

Truth softens or makes the heart bitter

Truth is the explosion of a situation

Nobody can stop the truth

Truth is often concealed

Searching for truth = path of justice

Truth speaks to all
Not only to doctors and lawyers

Truth is often fear

Truth has a pungent smell

Truth is not always breathable

Childhood = truth = surprise

Truth = discovery + response + certainty + sincerity + accuracy + visionary path

Truth is a seven-note chord

Truth is a long quest

Truth is the path to God

Truth = knowledge

Truth is anti-mendacity

Truth reveals

Truth = ontology of life

Truth = belief + evidence + certainty

Truth will never again be a half-truth

How many truths are there? = only one

Truth = wisdom + honesty + clarity

Beauty

$\mathcal{B}$eauty delights

Beauty is poetic violence

Beauty = pure pleasure

Is there absolute beauty?

Beauty is the heart's arrangement

Beauty is voluptuousness throughout the body

Beauty is immediate = it hates reason

Beauty = goodness

Beauty = simple lines

Beauty = grace + intoxication + poetry + truth

Fine arts are beautiful because they are beauty

Beauty = harmony

Beauty = splendor

Is beauty fashionable?
Of course not

Beauty is in us

Beauty is life-saving

Beauty is the dawn between heaven and earth

Beauty is profound appearance

Beauty does not like the functional

Beauty = a loving gesture

Beauty is the soft space of a landscape

Beauty is the art of living well

Beauty or happiness

Beauty is the abode of Being

I aspire to absolute beauty

Beauty is not superfluous

Beauty is always useful

Reality is the signifier and beauty the signified

Beauty reflects God

Beauty is divine irradiation

Beauty is encountering the world

Beauty = the experience of encounter

Beauty = desire to know the truth

Beauty = communicating with one's own emotion

Beauty = resonance of the heart

Time

Time passes like clouds

Time walks lightly

Time is that of a rose

No
Time is not an abyss = it is the locus of poetry

Time = life's pleasure

Time = suspended delight

Time = past + present + future = One

Time changes things

Is time a woman?
I will court her

Time = space + love + life + death + work + relativity +
geometric mind + subtle mind

In my hands time is a substance for plowing

I regulate time

Time is not money
It is a slow happiness

Time is measured by the heart

Time wants no clock

Time is against clepsydras

Time measures life

Time is neither short nor long

I live time = therefore I live life

I have my own time
That is why I keep it religiously

Time has no variables

Time is indivisible

Time is a three-time waltz

Time is not a stage

Sharing time is sharing life

There is no due time = there is lightning

I love solar time

Olden times are present times

Time is never biblical

Time does not go fast = it goes

I prefer cherry time
And almond time

I am time

We are time

Everyone is time

Color

The key to the world comes in color

A cry of joy
Is an explosion of the color red

Essence of color essence of energy

On the edge of life
The road has colors

Color is the spirit of things

Color = Total synthesis

Fantasy = colors

Abstraction = colors

Dream + life + space + dialogue + peace = colors

Clear shapes = light shattered = signs of color

Color has no time

Color = lightness of heart

Alchemy of life = colors of the rainbow

Color converses with sun and moon

An olive tree = colors of an azure sky

Childhood = poetry = colors

Esplanade of desires = that of colors

Color is the convergence of forms

Through color
I question the world

Color is the space of life

Color is resplendent

Beauty has no precise color

Color is a degree of light

Colors + art + beauty = an essential bond

Color is a necessity

The symbolism of colors accompanies our life

Letters are in color

Color has no decoration

Color is no ornament

Color is anti-violence

Light is the color of the world

Color is the language of joy

Color = music of life

Color = energy

Color is the evidence of love

Shape does not lack an internal color

Color = concentration of life = birth + life + death

Flowers

The stems of a bouquet of flowers
Are the pillars of the universe

Star = flower of the sky

Blue horizon = flowers of desire

Windows open the flowers of the world

Chimera of conscience = flowers on the path

Flowers = gnosis of the soul

Knowledge multiplies infinitely
In the flowers' corolla

Flowers are destiny's sign

I see a girl again = she reminds me of the flower of
youth

Flowers observe time

Flowers grow imagination

Flowers = magic of symbols

Flowers = musical jets of water

Flowers = cosmic vision

Flowers are truth and purity

Flowers = organization of beauty

Flowers = symbols of a garden

Flowers = anti-debacle of modernity

Flowers reassure

Flowers are a sweet horizon

Flowers = sense of tempered freedom

Flowers represent the first day of Creation

Flowers arouse the imagination

Flowers have an aesthetic value

The silence of flowers is the silence of the soul

Flowers are beautiful and useful

Flowers signal the course of time

Flowers are between heaven and earth

Flowers are a spiritual promise

Flowers signal impermanent temporality

Flowers open up a space for spring

A breath of life emanates from flowers

Floral arrangement = desire to live in beauty

Flowers = solemn hymn to life

Flowers = fragility and greatness of man

Bouquet of flowers = knowledge principle

The other

$\mathcal{E}$nlightening the other's voice = a sublime task

Listen to the presence of the other = the music of life

Debacle of the other = debacle of the self

Other = cross-culture + life

Diversifying the world = testament to the other

Mixing people = my ideal

Other = plural man

Other = voice of illumination

The other speaks the language of language

The other intercedes

The other is on fire

The other is my brother

Other = unity

The other enlightens

The other crosses the world

Other = bridge of hearts

Other = past and future

Other = meditative Being

Other = scars of history = healed by love

Other = integration

Other = community

Other = memory + origin + civilization

Other = voices are all equal

Other = crossroads of civilization

The other is the symbol of humanism

The other listens = let us listen to him

Other = fraternity + understanding

My ego and alter ego = two children of the same star

Other = my identity

No antagonism between me and the other

The voice of the other gazes at the purity of its reflection

Other = round-trip

Other = back and forth

Other = exchange

Other = no frontiers

Other = star + work + sacrifices + travel

The other loves

The other thinks

The other thirsts

The other is the bohemian of the other

Other = desert + sea + love

The other prays

The other breathes

The other knows the taste of death

The other crosses my threshold

The other is a gardener of love

Other = real life

Science

Science = magic of the world

Science is the horizon of progress

Science shows the signs of the universe

Science loves the firmament

Science = dawn's line

Science = love + research + life + passion + poetry

Science is the stone's water

Science perceives color in a constellation

Science is a rose of the depths

Science tells how

Science = window to the earth's secret

Science = the awakening of dormancy

Science = heaven's road

Science erases clouds

Science announces the future

Science is the rise of Ideal

Science is an illumination

Science questions

Science clarifies

Science is not obscure

Science searches infinity

Science is a torch

Science tells of reason and the heart

Science is blood red

Science = Kepler + Galileo + Einstein + Spallanzani
+ Marconi + Volta + Rimbaud + Apollinaire + Ungaretti
+ Bonnefoy + Stétié + Luzi

Science is this and that

Science is the poetry of algebra

Science knows letters and colors

Science = levity

Science is infinity

Science = ego versus the world

Science = holding a light

Science = hymn to the Lord

Science = positive anxiety

Science = alliance with the universe

Science is the freedom to think and to invent

Science goes deep

Science is words and symbols

Science is project and emotion

Science = a new humanism

Science will save us
Alongside poetry

Science is the alchemy of love

Light

Voice of light = voice of constellation

Light = procession of oriental dancers

Light = prophecy of wheat

Light = articulates the original garden

Light is the space of hope

Light is the groove of a trace

Light = wandering the universe

Light = ontology of memory

Hoping for enlightenment = light upon light

Wisdom is a heavenly light

Light is asceticism up above

The silence of light is the word of the Angel

Light is the infinite star

Light = spiral arabesque

Light mixes fullness and the void

Light is the result of an ordeal

Central light = crystal vase

Eternity illuminates the light

Light is revealed through the sky's alphabet

Light is the writing of dreams

Light is a blue jasmine

Light = light of hope

Light shows the way

Light is an enigma

Light is my mother's son

Light = blue stones + diamond + lamp + prairie + snow
+ rose + awakening + future

Light has red wings

Light is as immense as the heart

Light stokes the fire

Light is the abyss of dreams

Light = sunbathing

Light is a materialized chimera

Light opens the Book of Books

Light comes from Paradise

Light does not burn

Light is the infinite horizon

Light is a seedling of vision

Light is the crossroads of destiny

Light never cries

Light brings a time for love

Light turns on the morning's lamp

Light is a flowery fire

Light is in colorland

Light comes from the locus of loci

Light is timeless

Life

$\mathcal{I}$ shape my life day by day
Just like I shape my words

Life has carried me away like a rose

June 24, 1942 gave me life

Life is not birth and death = it is always belonging to
poetry

Life = our destiny's course

Life = creation

Life = invention

Life = Poetry

Life embraces me at all times

Life = love = travel

I live at home
Therefore in my life

Life = body + soul

Life = long-term thought + possible death

Life = freedom + daring + projecting + searching +
dreaming

Life = living

Life = joie de vivre
Despite death

I have but one goal = living at the center of the universe

Life = existence + fate + destiny + lived time + hope

My life is in poetry

Love's sorrows = life's bread

Life = biography of our light

What life am I living?
That of a poet

Private life or public?
No matter

Provided my heart is there

I always look at life squarely

I love life through rose-colored glasses

Life = a blue pathway

Life flows like a torrent of water

Life travels in an instant

Life = succession of continua

I tell my life in poetry

I am life

Life = ongoing course

Life is erased and reborn

Life fades
I rebuild it

Life is the human condition

Life = expectancy

Life is here and now

Life is hope

Each moment of life is a source of pleasure

Rhythm of days = rhythm of life
Life has three dimensions = past + present + future

Life is the horizon of Being

Life = promise of travel + transfiguration

Life is the labyrinth of time

Life is a spiritual duration

Life = love of destiny

Life = transcendence + magic

Eternity of life = time of freedom

After each passing life begins anew

One lives to live
In life

Life of the stars = my life

One does not fight against life

Life is not uninhabitable

Life = breathing movement

My life = my blood

Life = seismography of time

Life = a path of wonders

Other French Poetry by the Author

La lampe des choses, avec 4 acryliques de Jacques Clauzel, Gal- largues-le-Montueux, Éditions À Travers, 1999, 32 p. Artist manuscript. 8 copies.

Carnet d'étincelles, Bergerac, Les Amis de la Poésie, 2001, 60 p. Prix La Toison d'Or, Bergerac 2003.

Jean Vendome joaillier de la pierre, photos de Raphaêl Vendome, Fasano, Schena, 2001, 64 p. 8 color illustrations.

Corps illuné, dessins de Michele Damiani, Rochefort-du- Gard, Alain Lucien Benoit, 2001, 32 p.

Paris poème, version en français par l'auteur, Fasano, Schena, 2001, 90 p.

Écritures japonaises. Artist manuscript, 2 color notebooks, 16 p.

Écritures des pierres, photos de Raphaêl Vendome, Fasano, Schena, 2002, 96 p. 42 illustrations.

Lianes bleues. Poème, avec 18 aquarelles de Michele Damiani, Fasano, Bergerac, Schena, Les Amis de la Poésie, 2002, 240 p. Limited artist edition, 400 copies signed by the artist and the poet.

Traces de parole, eaux-fortes de Dominique Médard, Fasano, Schena, 2002, 96 p. Limited artist edition, 126 copies numbered from 1 to 100 and from A to Z.

Paris Poèmes, Colomiers, Encres vives, 2003, 14 p.

Le chemin de l'Un, dessins de Dominique Médard, Tours, Le Livre pauvre, 2003, 8 p. Artist manuscript. 7 copies.

Litanies de l'Un, dessins de Vincenzo Viti, Rochefort du Gard, Alain Lucien Benoit, 2003.

Le fils du vent, Fasano, Schena, 2004, 90 p.

Les sept portes, eaux-fortes de Dominique Médard, Fasano,

Schena, 2004, 72 p. Limited artist edition, 126 copies numbered from 1 to 100 and from A to Z.

Mes nuages, photographies de Jacques Clauzel, Fasano, Schena, 2005, 128 p. Limited artist edition. 326 copies numbered from 1 to 300 and from I to XXVI.

Cicatrices de poésie, Fasano, Schena, 2005, 104 p.

Espérance. Poème, Paris, Lanore, 2006, 96 p.

Paris en quatrains, Paris, Lanore, 2006, 96 p. Prix de l'Académie de Versailles 2007.

À huis ouvert, Colomiers, « Encres vives », n. 334, mars 2007, 20 p.

Rimbaud ou la Maison des Ailleurs, photographies de Jean-Marie Lecompte, préface d'Alain Tourneux, Fasano, Schena, 2007, 64 p.

Loches mon amour, gravures de Ferdinand Dubreuil, préface de Pierre Bourgeade, Fasano, Paris, Schena - Le Jardin de la Création, 2008, 84 p.

Auréole de la rose, couleurs de Dominique Médard, 2008, 16 p. Artist manuscript. 15 copies.

Dictionnaire des citations de mon cœur. Alphabet poétique, préface d'Alain Rey, Paris, Alain Baudry et Cie, 2008, 182 p.

La Voix Lumière, Paris, Éditions du Cygne, 2009, 124 p. 100 copies with CD containing five texts put to music by Éric Guilleton.

Calligraphies de l'alphabet, en collaboration avec Ghani Alani, Fasano, Paris, Schena, Alain Baudry et Cie, 2009. *Aiguilles d'arabesque. Poèmes pour ma Figure*, dessins de Michele Damiani, Paris, Éditions du Cygne, 2009.

Le sang du sel, dessins de Michele Damiani, Paris, Éditions du Cygne, 2010, 102 p.

Je la vie. Œuvres poétiques, préface de Pierre Brunel, Fasano. Paris, Schena, Éditions du Cygne, 2010, 2 vol., 1166 + XX p. [Compilation of poetry published through 2010]. Prix

Dante, Cénacle européen francophone de Poésie, Arts et Lettres - Paris, 2010.

Dictionnaire d'aphoripoésie de Ah ! à Zut ! Aphorismes pour bien vivre, préface d'Alain Rey, Paris, Éditions du Cygne, 2010, 208 p.

Aube, dessins de Michele Damiani, Paris, L'Harmattan, 2010, 76 p.

La Beauté. Une Harmonie autre du Monde, dessins de Michele Damiani, Paris, Éditions du Cygne, 2011, 158 p.

Carrefours, Paris, L'Harmattan, 2011, 128 p.

Là haut l'amandier, dessins de Michele Damiani, Paris, Éditions du Cygne, 2011, 94 p.

Voyage des mots, dessins de Michele Damiani, Paris, Alain Baudry et Cie, 2012, 84 p.

La nuit le passage, préface de Constantin Frosin, Paris, Éditions du Cygne, 2012, 116 p.

Les portes bleues. Voyage au Maroc, Paris, L'Harmattan, 2012, 86 p.

Sonnets intuitistes, préface d'Éric Sivry, illustrations d'Alain Béral, Roger Gonnet, Laudine Jacobée, Simon Lambrey, Pierre Ligou, Jean-Claude Pommery, Paris, Alain Baudry et Cie, 2012, 164 p.

Géométries d'enfance. Poèmes-vers, Paris, Éditions du Cygne, 2012, 112 p.

Bonjour poème !, Paris, L'Harmattan, 2013, 106 p.

Peintres de la modernité, Paris, Éditions du Cygne, 2013, 114 p. *Rimes parisiennes. Rime parigine*, Tableaux-Poèmes [di] Michele Damiani, traduzione [di] Mario Selvaggio, Fasano - Paris, Schena - Alain Baudry et Cie 2013, 24 p.

Chansons de Paris. Canzoni per Parigi, tableaux-poèmes [di] Michele Damiani, introduzione, traduzione e cura [di] Mario Selvaggio, Roma, Edizioni Universitarie Romane, 2014, 282 p.

Passages. Chansons de Paris, tableaux-poèmes de Michele Damiani, Paris, Éditions Tensing, 2014, 184 p. With a CD contening poems put to music by Étienne Champollion and sung by Damien Roquetty and Marianne Croux [and later by Océane Champollion].

Je la femme ! / Woman I am, dessins et traduction en anglais de Vivian O'Shaughnessy, avec le texte original en regard, Paris, Éditions Tensing, 2014, 250 p.

Éclairs d'Infini. Lampi d'infinito, introduzione, traduzione e cura di Mario Selvaggio. Appendix: *Rimes parisiennes*, tradotte in lingua serba da Marija Šuva ki, postface di Éric Sivry, Roma, Edizioni Universitarie Romane, 2014, 146 p.

Chansons de Montmartre, illustrations de Midani [M'barka], Paris, Éditions Thierry Sajat, 2014, 134 p.

Photoécritures, en collaboration avec Thierry Delaballe, Fasano, Paris, Schena, Alain Baudry et Cie, 2014, 36 p.

Le livre. Éloge de la page-papier, photographies de Pino Addante, Paris, Éditions du Cygne, 2014, 132 p.

Le train de la vie qui va, [texte orginal en regard], traduction en italien de Mario Selvaggio, tableaux-poèmes de Michele Damiani, Paris, Alain Baudry & Cie, 2014, 128 p.

42 + 7 visions, Paris, Éditions du Cygne, 2015, 88 p.

Je la Vie. Œuvres poétiques, introduction de Pierre Brunel, Fasano - Paris, Schena - Éditions du Cygne, 2015, vol. III, 852 p.

L'abri du berger, préface de Constantin Frosin, Paris, Galerie-Librairie Racine, 2016, 102 p.

Aphorismes poétiques, Paris, Éditions du Cygne, 2016, 112 p.

La nature nous appelle. Infographies. Ode, Paris, Éditions Tensing, 2016, 118 p.

Le vrai portrait d'Alain Béral, Artist manuscript, 2016, 32 p., one copy.

Tour à tour des flaques, Paris, Éditions Tensing, 2016, 94 p.

Je suis Orient, encres de Patrick Navaï, Beaufour-Druval, Beaufour-Druval, La Feuille de thé, 2017, 74 p.

Onomatopoésie, préface d'Alain Rey, tableaux-poèmes d'Alain Béral, Paris, Le Nouvel Athanor, 2017, 156 p.

Ce fut une pierre, Paris, Lanore, 2017, 112 p.

L'olivier ou L'arbre de la vie, tableaux-poèmes d'Alain Béral, Paris, Le Nouvel Athanor, 2017, 136 p.

Psaumes du temps, Paris, Éditions du Cygne, 2017, 86 p.

Mon rêve à Cordoue, avec un Hommage à Grenade / Mi sueño en Cordoba con homenaje incluido a Granada, traduction et introduction de / traducción y introdución de Rafael Ruiz Álvarez, Paris, L'Harmattan, 2017, 180 p.

Manifeste pour la poésie du troisième millénaire, traduction en anglais R.-L. Étienne Barnett, traduction en italien Mario Selvaggio, traduction en espagnol Encarnación Medina Arjona, Alberobello - Paris, AGA - L'Harmattan, 2018, 48 p.

Éclats, collages de Patrick Navaï, Alberobello - Paris, AGA - L'Harmattan, 2018, 144 p.

Reviennent mes pas, Paris, Éditions du Cygne, 2019, 98 p.

Le hasard la liberté, Alberobello - Paris, AGA - L'Harmattan, 2019, 112 p.

Étymologies, collages de Patrick Navaï et préface d'Alain Rey, Paris, AGA-L'Harmattan, 2019.

Dialogue-monologue avec Charles Baudelaire, in *Baudelaire ou Le corps de la Douleur*, sous la direction de Giovanni Dotoli et Mario Selvaggio, Alberobello - Paris, Editrice AGA - L'Harmattan, 2019, 153-166 p.

Figuration de la lumière, photographies de Thierry Delaballe, Alberobello - Paris, Editrice AGA - L'Harmattan, 2019, 116 p.

L'autre c'est moi, photographies de Thierry Delaballe, Alberobello - Paris, Editrice AGA - L'Harmattan, 2019, 104 p.

L'autre, mon frère, tableaux-poèmes de Patrick Navaï, musique d'Étienne Champollion, Alberobello - Paris, Editrice AGA

- L'Harmattan, 2019, 112 p.

Symphonie en bleu, photographies de Thierry Delaballe, musique d'Étienne Champollion, Alberobello - Paris, Editrice AGA - L'Harmattan, 2019, 156 p.

L'âme du monde, Alberobello - Paris, Editrice AGA - L'Harmattan, 2020, 84 p.

Clic sur l'éternel, Paris - Alberobello, L'Harmattan - Editrice AGA, 2020, 196 p.

Maths = Infini, Paris - Alberobello, L'Harmattan - Editrice AGA, 2020, 112 p.

Je la Vie. Œuvres poétiques, volume IV, *2014-2016*, Paris - Alberobello, L'Harmattan - Editrice AGA, 2020, 808 p.

Je la Vie. Œuvres poetiques, volume V, *2017-2020*, Paris - Alberobello, L'Harmattan - AGA Editrice, 2020, 840 p.

Fenêtres de Paris / Finestre di Parigi. Tableaux-Poèmes, [texte de G. Dotoli, tableau-poèmes de Michele Damiani], Paris - Alberobello, L'Harmattan - AGA Editrice, 2020, 26 p. + 7 tableaux-poèmes.

Fenêtres, Paris - Alberobello, L'Harmattan - AGA Editrice, 2021, 128 p.

Dialogue avec Dante, musique d'Étienne Champollion, Paris - Alberobello, L'Harmattan - AGA Editrice, 2021, 168 p.

Partir, peintures de Patrick Navaï, Paris - Alberobello, L'Harmattan - AGA Editrice, 2021, 2022, 124 p.

L'invisible, Paris - Alberobello, L'Harmattan - AGA Editrice, 2022, 68 p.

Lumière & magie du noir, en collaboration avec Thierry Delaballe, Paris - Alberobello, L'Harmattan - AGA Editrice, 2022, 152 p.

Paris Poésie, Paris - Alberobello, L'Harmattan - AGA Editrice, 2022, 376 p.

Épopée, encres de Michele Damiani, Paris - Alberobello, L'Harmattan - AGA, « L'Orizzonte n. 187 », 2023, 92 p.

TABLE DES MATIÈRES

Achevé d'imprimer en mai 2023
sur les presses de
AGA Arti Grafiche Alberobello
70011 Alberobello (I - Ba)
Contrada Popoleto, nc - tél. 00390804322044
www.editriceaga.it - info@editriceaga.it

Dépôt légal : mai 2023
Copyright L'Harmattan et AGA

L'ORIZZONTE

Collana fondata e diretta da
Giovanni Dotoli, Encarnación Medina Arjona, Mario Selvaggio
noria.info aga.lorizzonte lharmattan.lorizzonte

27. Alexandrine-Sophie de Bawr, *Storie per ragazzi (La moneta da cinquecento centesimi - Il vecchio cieco)*, introduzione, traduzione e cura di Martina Matteu, illustrazioni [di] Bertall, 2018, 124 p.

28. Louis Lemercier de Neuville, *Storie abracadabranti*, introduzione, traduzione e cura di Valeria Aresu, illustrazioni [di] Donato Selvaggio, 2018, 104 p.

29. Giovanni Dotoli, *Dialogo con Padre Pio. Poema-teatro in 5 atti*, composizioni musicali di Étienne Champollion, 2018, 120 p.

30. Giovanni Dotoli - Mario Selvaggio, *Vertige frangé. Jean Laugier, avec une anthologie du poète*, 2018, 124 p.

31. Carolyne Cannella, *Instants. Tercets - Hommage au Japon*, préface de Giovanni Dotoli, 2018, 88 p.

32. Giovanni Dotoli, *Connaissance en poche ou De l'encyclopédie*, 2018, 140 p.

33. Rachida Madani, *The Story Can Wait. A novel*, english translation and introductory essay by M. J. Muratore, 2020, 188 p.

34. Éric Sivry, *Faustine*, 2018, 92 p.

35. Aim-A, *Mère si ... à corps père dû. Manifeste*, introduction de Valentin de Carbonnières, préface de Giovanni Dotoli, 2018, 168 p.

36. Mario Selvaggio, *A vele spiegate nel Mediterraneo. Identità e nomadismo in Bouraoui*. À paraître 2021.

37. Giovanni Dotoli, *Cosa è successo?*, illustrazioni [di] Donato Selvaggio, 2018, 104 p.

38. *Poésie et poétique dans l'Encyclopédie. Six entrées*, par Mario Selvaggio, 2018, 212 p.

39. Giovanni Dotoli - Éric Jacobée-Sivry - Rosamaria Pau - Mario Selvaggio, sous la direction de, *Dans les mains du monde. Hommage à Jean Laugier*, Actes du Colloque de l'Université de Cagliari (le 20 octobre 2018), 2018, 180 p.

40. Jacques Herman - Maria Zaki, *Les signes de l'absence. Poésie entrecroisée / I segni dell'assenza. Intrecci poetici*, introduction et traduction en italien par Mario Selvaggio, 2018, 104 p.

41. René Le Bars, *Harmonies. Poèmes*, dessins de Brigitte Simon, 2018, 124 p.

42. M. J. Muratore, *Weapons of Word-Play in " Une vie de boy " and " La Rue Cases-Nègres »*. À paraître 2021.

43. Ilda Tomas, *À l'infini…*, 2018, 220 p.

44. Giovanni Dotoli - Mario Selvaggio - Éric Jacobée-Sivry - Jocelyne Verguin, sous la direction de, *L'Encyclopédie de Diderot et d'Alembert et les projets encyclopédistes du XVIIIᵉ siècle*, Actes de la Journée de Meaux, Lycée Bossuet 19 mars 2018, 2018, 108 p.

45. Giovanni Dotoli, *Dictionnaire poétique et thématique de l'intuition*, 2019, 332 p.

46. Elisa Tordella, *Shakespeare in Canada: A Journey into the Canadian Soul*, foreword by Giovanni Dotoli, 2019, 304 p.

47. Susan Petrilli - Augusto Ponzio, *Dizionario, Enciclopedia, Traduzione fra César Chesneau Dumarsais e Umberto Eco*, 2019, 160 p.

48. Frédéric-Gaël Theuriau, *La médecine narrative dans les nouvelles humanités médicales. Dialectique du médecin, de la maladie et du malade*, 2019, 92 p.

49. Olivier Furon-Bazan, *Méli-Mélo. Recueil et essais poétiques*, dessins de Brigitte Simon, 2019, 152 p.

50. Giovanni Dotoli, *Étymologies*, collages de Patrick Navaï, préface de Alain Rey, 2019, 168 p.

51. Paola Salerni, *Aspects du lexique et du discours de l'Administration française au fil des siècles. Le système des charges, des lois, du territoire*, 2021, 444 p.

52. *Sur la route de la poésie et de la lumière*, 77 poèmes et 17 illustrations pour le 77ᵉ anniversaire de Giovanni Dotoli, sous la direction de Mario Selvaggio, 2019, 168 p.

53. Thierry Delaballe & Giovanni Dotoli, *Figuration de la lumière*, 2019, 116 p.

54. Giovanni Dotoli, *Phrase, logique, discours, figement*, 2019, 140 p.

55. *Arabesques de lumière. Rencontre avec la poésie de Giovanni Dotoli*, Actes du Colloque international, Sala della Loggia - Nuovo Maschio Angioino, Naples, le 23 mars

2019, sous la direction de Maria Leo & Mario Selvaggio, 2019, 168 p.

56. *Baudelaire ou Le corps de la Douleur*, sous la direction de Giovanni Dotoli et Mario Selvaggio, 2019, 268 p.

57. Ilda Tomas, *Lexique affolé d'amour*, préface de Giovanni Dotoli, 2019, 224 p.

58. Giovanni Dotoli, *Défense et illustration de la littérature*, 2019, 180 p.

59. Giovanni Dotoli, *Défense et illustration de la poésie*, 2019, 264 p.

60. Giovanni Dotoli & Mario Selvaggio, *Le vampire dans la poésie française. XIXe - XXe siècles. Anthologie*, préface de Alain Rey, illustrations de Emma Virginia Puggioni, 2019, 480 p.

61. Salvatore Gucciardo, *Ombres et Lumières*, préface de Giovanni Dotoli, 2019, 116 p.

62. Giovanni Dotoli & Thierry Delaballe, *L'autre c'est moi*, 2019, 104 p.

63. Encarnación Medina Arjona, *La hora azul. El París de Olavide*, 2019, 272 p.

64. René Corona, *Passage du temps et des courants. L'imagination ô savoir ! Le spectacle du monde : pour un micro-imaginaire poétique*, 2019, 408 p.

65. Éric Jacobée-Sivry, *Une autre conception de l'autre. Penser l'autre au fil des siècles*, 2019, 72 p.

66. Giovanni Dotoli, *Défense et illustration de la langue française et de la francophonie*, 2019, 224 p.

67. Giovanni Dotoli, *L'autre, mon frère*, tableaux-poèmes de Patrick Navaï, musique de Étienne Champollion, 2019, 112 p.

68. René Corona, *Croquer le marmot sous l'ombre*, 2019, 216 p.

69. René Corona, *Sortilèges de la retenue sous le bleu indigo de la pluie*, 2019, 128 p.

70. Giovanni Dotoli & Thierry Delaballe, *Symphonie en bleu*, musique de Étienne Champollion, 2019, 156 p.

71. Michel Arouimi, *Histoire de l'art*, 2019, 152 p.

72. Michele Damiani & Giovanni Dotoli, *Le maître de l'azur / Il maestro d'azzurro.*

Tableaux-Poèmes, 2019, 16 + 20 p.

73. Giovanni Dotoli, *Le mot* démocratie *dans le dictionnaire*, 2019, 180 p.

74. Encarnación Medina Arjona, *Trente poèmes d'amour*, dessins de Michele Damiani, 2019, 92 p.

75. Giovanni Dotoli, *Il fiume della vita*, tableaux-poèmes di Loredana Cacucciolo, 2019, 132 p.

76. *PresenzeSilenti Arte Contemporanea*, a cura di Loredana Cacucciolo, con la collaborazione di Marisa D'Agostino, testo critico di Rosalinda Romanelli, 2019, 56 p.

77. Christine Boubal, *Gai ou triste. Mosaïques d'une vie*, illustrations de Sakoto Mori, 2020, 80 p.

78. Giovanni Dotoli, *La paix un bien commun*, 2020, 148 p.

79. Rita Pacilio, *Les nervures de la violette*, traduction de l'italien de Françoise Lenoir, 2020, 64 p.

80. Mario Selvaggio, *Vie, identité, temps dans la poésie de Giovanni Dotoli*, 2020, 148 p.

81. *Emozioni. L'altro lato del sapere. Epistemologia Formazione Creatività / Emocje. Druga strona wiedzy. Epistemologia Kształcenie Kreatywność*, a cura di / pod redakcją Diana Del Mastro - Wiesław Dyk, vol. 2, 2019, 380 p.

82. Fulvia Fiorino Dotoli, *Una vita, romanzo*, disegni di Michele Damiani, 2020, 190 p.

83. Brice Grudina, *Insonnia. Rehab*, prefazione di Mario Selvaggio, 2020, 132 p.

84. Giovanni Dotoli, *Défense et illustration de la musique*, tableaux-poèmes de Michele Damiani, 2020, 336 p.

85. Giovanni Dotoli, *L'âme du monde*, 2020, 84 p.

86. *Symbolum. Mito Immaginario Realtà*, a cura di / pod redakcją Diana Del Mastro, 2020, 372 p.

87. *À l'aube de la mémoire. Identité et vie dans la poésie de Giovanni Dotoli*, Actes du Colloque international, sous la direction de Maria Leo et Mario Selvaggio, Avellino, le 18 janvier 2020, 2020, 196 p.

88. Giovanni Dotoli, *Zola écrivain du XXIe siècle*, 2020, 100 p.

89. Thierry Delaballe & Giovanni Dotoli, *Clic sur l'éternel*, 2020, 196 p.

90. Mario Selvaggio, *Alchimie poetiche*, 2020, 196 p.

91. *Padre Pio*, testi di Giovanni Dotoli, composizioni musicali di Étienne Champollion, 2020, 82 p.

92. Javier Del Prado Biezma, *Le lavoir au lézard bleu*, 2020, 102 p.

93. Lydia de Haro Hernández et Jean-Paul Socard, *Défense et Illustration des femmes de lettres en France au XIXᵉ siècle*. Réédition critique du texte de Georges de Peyrebrune " Jupiter et les Bas-bleus » paru dans le recueil *Celui qui revient*. Paris, P. Ollendorff, 1894, 2020, 280 p.

94. Giovanni Dotoli, *Maths ≅ Infini*, 2020, 112 p.

95. Giovanni Dotoli, *L'œil de Furetière ou De l'universalité de la langue*, 2020, 132 p.

96. Giovanni Dotoli, *Dictionnaire, langage, langue française, vie. Entretiens avec Alain Rey*, 2020, 148 p.

97. Giovanni Dotoli, *Je la Vie. Œuvres poétiques*, volume IV, *2014-2016*, 2020, 808 p.

98. Giovanni Dotoli, *Je la Vie. Œuvres poétiques*, volume V, *2017-2020*, 2020, 840 p.

99. Christophe Boubal, *France rose fanée dans le bouquet du monde*, 2020, 456 p.

100. Giovanni Dotoli, *La Rosa del Punto*, volume III, *2011-2020*, 2020, 600 p.

101. Sophie Laroque-Texier, *Ô la terre !*, encres et gravures de Hiroko Hori, avec traduction en italien de Francesco Bruno, 2021, 64 + 16 p.

102. Giovanni Dotoli & Michele Damiani, *Fenêtres de Paris. Finestre di Parigi. Tableaux-Poèmes*, 2020, 26 p. + 7 Tableaux-Poèmes.

103. Rome Deguergue, *La part des femmes suivi de &Ros(e) noir(e)*, 2020, 420 p.

104. Encarnación Medina Arjona, *Arbres, arbres. Poèmes*, 2021, 84 p.

105. Giovanni Dotoli, *Les artistes italiens d'après André Suarès*, 2021, 196 p.

106. Giovanni Dotoli, *Fenêtres*, Tableaux-Poèmes de Michele Damiani, 2021, 128 p.

107. Brice Grudina, *Canto ribelle*, prefazione [di] Mario Selvaggio, 2021, 164 p.

108. Michel Arouimi, *Le vraie vie des objets*, 2021, 104 p.

109. Sophie Laroque-Texier, *À la lune !*, encres de Daniel Pontoreau, traduction en italien de Francesco Bruno, 2021, 60 + 12 p.

110. *Symbolum. Terra Mater Materia*, a cura di Diana Del Mastro e Angela Giallongo, 2020, 440 p.

111. Giovanni Dotoli, *Lire Alain Rey*, préface de Salah Mejri, 2021, 228 p.

112. *Pagine di periferia. Loredana Cacucciolo*, 2021, 32 p.

113. Giovanni Dotoli, *Dialogue avec Dante*, musique [d'] Étienne Champollion, 2021, 168 p.

114. Giovanni Dotoli, *Dialogo con Dante*, musica [di] Étienne Champollion, traduzione dal francese di Mario Selvaggio, illustrazioni [di] Giulia Spano, 2021, 184 p.

115. Maria Zaki, *Au dédale de l'âme / Nel labirinto dell'anima*, prefazione, traduzione e cura [di] Mario Selvaggio, con un inchiostro di Giulia Spano, 2021, 152 p.

116. *Le poète au XXIᵉ siècle. Nouveau monde, nouvelle mode*, Actes de la Journée d'étude internationale. Faculté des Lettres - Sorbonne Université, Paris, 13 février 2021, sous la direction de Giovanni Dotoli, Bernard Franco, Nicolas Grenier, Mario Selvaggio, avec une encre de Giulia Spano, 2021, 188 p.

117. Daniel-Henri Pageaux, *Esquisses parisiennes. Lectures de Mérimée*, 2021, 176 p.

118. Sophie Laroque-Texier, *Sur Pontoreau, pierres étoilées*, 2021, 100 p.

119. Arthur Rimbaud, *Le Bateau ivre*, édition d'artiste par Giovanni Dotoli, traduction poétique en italien Mario

Selvaggio, tableaux inspirés par le poème Gérard Beaulieu, Michel Bénard, Alain Béral, Michele Damiani, Salvatore Gucciardo, Éliane Hurtado, Simon Lambrey, Patrick Navaï, Jean-Claude Pommery, Roland Souchon, Giulia Spano, 2021, 54 + 16 + 44 p.

120. René Corona , *Nos dicos sentimentaux*, 2021, 280 p.

121. Giovanni Dotoli, *Alain Rey. Bibliographie complète* et *Lexique thématique*, 2021, 272 p.

122. Sophie Laroque-Texier, *Haïku*, encres de Henri Texier, 2021, 92 p.

123. M. J. Muratore, *Aux carrefours du labyrinthe. Narration et fragmentation chez Assia Djebar, Sabiha Khemir, Rachida Madani*, 2021, 144 p.

124. Giovanni Dotoli, *La pensée socialiste française de Saint-Simon à Péguy, Anthologie*, 2021, 932 p.

125. Séda Azadiguian, *Rêves de Soleil*, dessins [de] Gabie Audousset, 2021, 64 p.

126. René Corona, *Chansons et imaginaire. Pour une poétique fredonnée* suivi du *Cinoche pour tous*, 2021, 424 p.

127. Giovanni Dotoli, *Bovarysme et féminisme*, 2021, 120 p.

128. Daniel-Henri Pageaux, *Passages de l'écrit*, 2021, 176 p.

129. *Rimbaud. Le Bateau ivre a 150 ans*, sous la direction de Pierre Brunel, Giovanni Dotoli, Arnaud Santolini, Mario Selvaggio, 2021, 328 p.

130. Pierre Leroux, *Doctrine de l'Humanité. Aphorismes*, édition établie et présentée par Mario Selvaggio, 2021, 96 p.

131. *Soleil des Antipodes. Mélanges offerts à Mohamed Aziza / Shams Nadir*, À l'initiative de Giovanni Dotoli et Othman Ben Taleb, 2021, 528 p.

132. Giovanni Dotoli, *Le livre entre papier et numérique*, 2021, 168 p.

133. *L'argent du libertinage*, Actes de la journée d'étude virtuelle du 31 juillet 2021, sous la direction de Eric Turcat, 2021, 188 p.

134. Ridha Bourkhis, *Un ritorno al paese del buon Dio*, traduzione in italiano di Maria Teresa Fiore, 2021, 140 p.

135. Giovanni Dotoli, *Léon Bloy et l'argent. Christianisme, marxisme, socialisme, anarchisme*, 2022, 228 p.

136. Sophie Laroque-Texier, *Essere poeta*, 2021, 40 p.

137. Diana del Mastro, *Passages. épistémologie, esthétique, langage dans l'itinéraire scientifique et spirituel de Pavel A. Florenskij*, 2021, 148 p.

138. Angelo Rella, *"Voleur de feu ». Fede, infanzia e nostalgia nella poetica di Giovanni Dotoli*, 2021, 144 p.

139. Giovanni Dotoli, *«Le Voyage» de Baudelaire. Un poème-clé*, 2022, 188 p.

140. Mario Selvaggio, *L'entrée* Grammaire *dans l'*Encyclopédie *de Diderot et d'Alembert*, 2022, 132 p.

141. Corentin Fernagut, *Avant l'aube*, préface de Laurent Desvoux-D'Yrek, 2022, 100 p.

142. Charles Brion, *Poèmes*, 2022, 132 p.

143. Giovanni Dotoli, *Lampi di segni*, 2022, 84 p.

144. Charles Baudelaire, *Le Voyage*, édition d'artiste par Giovanni Dotoli, traduction poétique en italien [par] Mario Selvaggio, traduction en chinois [par] Lichao Zhu, traduction en arabe [par] Béchir Ouerhani, tableaux et sculptures inspirés par le poème [d']Étienne Fatras, Michele Damiani, Franceleine Debellefontaine, Gérard Beaulieu, Jean-Claude Bemben, Paul Kichilov, Martine Dinet, Agnès Giudici (Giuco), Éliane Hurtado, Michel Bénard, Alain Béral, Salvatore Gucciardo, Patrick Navaï, Roland Souchon, 2022, 98 + 32 + 64 p.

145. Filomena Juncker, *Échos du silence dans l'œuvre en prose de Maria Ondina Br* 2022, 516 p.

146. *Il giardino di là del mare. Poesie e racconti di Maria Gabriella Adamo*, a cura di René Corona, 2022, 232 p.

147. Henriette-France Lafargue, *Au cœur de la langue de Giovanni Dotoli*, 2022, 160 p.

148. Giovanni Dotoli, *Partir*, peintures de Patrick Navaï, 2022, 124 p.

149. Georges de Peyrebrune, *De Fouillis-les-Oies à Paris*, suivi de *Un singulier voyage, une représentation cocasse de la France sous le Second Empire*, par Jean-Paul Socard, préface de Jean-Luc Buard, 2022, 276 p.

150. Brice Grudina, *Luci d'ombre*, prefazione di Giovanni Dotoli, 2022, 176 p.

151. Thierry Delaballe & Giovanni Dotoli, *Vol de feu*, 2022, 108 p.

152. *Les formes de la poésie*, sous la direction de Giovanni Dotoli, Bernard Franco, Encarnación Medina Arjona, Mario Selvaggio, 2022, 248 p.

153. Arnaud de Champris, *Borges, ou Les Labyrinthes du Verbe. Système de la littérature. Contribution à l'étude du cosmopolitisme littéraire de Jorge Luis Borges et introduction à son méta-texte*, préface de Pierre Brunel, 2022, 308 p.

154. Fulvia Fiorino, *In cucina tra salute e tradizione*, prefazione di Marisa Adduci, 2022, 168 p.

155. Giovanni Dotoli, *Il libro cartaceo nell'era digitale*, edizione italiana a cura di Mario Selvaggio, prefazione di Gianfranco Dioguardi, 2022, 180 p.

156. *Notre Ilda*, sous la direction de María de los Ángeles Hernández Gómez, avec la collaboration de Giovanni Dotoli, 2022, 188 p.

157. Giovanni Dotoli, *Liberté et droits de l'homme*, 2022, 220 p.

158. Daniel-Henri Pageaux, *Bajo el signo de Proteo. Ensayos de literatura general y comparada*, 2002, 172 p.

159. *L'héritage de Senghor*, préface [de] Moustapha Niasse, Président de l'Assemblée nationale du Sénégal, conclusion [d']Hélène Carrère d'Encausse, Secrétaire perpétuel de l'Académie française, coordination [de] Mohamed Aziza, Alban Bogeat, Benjamin Boutin, Giovanni Dotoli, Michèle Guillaume-Hofnung, 2022, 362 p.

160. Giovanni Dotoli, *Oltre*, 2022, 76 p.

161. Giovanni Dotoli, *L'invisible*, 2022, 68 p.

162. *Il potere della lingua. Argomentazione, propaganda, persuasione*, a cura di Mariadomenica Lo Nostro e Rosaria Minervini, 2022, 260 p.

163. Mario Selvaggio, *Roman et texte de voyage. Des espaces polyphoniques*, 2022, 92 p.

164. Thierry Delaballe & Giovanni Dotoli, *Lumière & magie du noir*, 2022, 152 p.

165. M. J. Muratore, *Stilled voices unmuted. The poetics of postcolonial silence*, 2022, 140 p.

166. *Cent ans. Conférences du centenaire des Cours de civilisation française de la Sorbonne*, sous la direction de Bernard Franco, 2022, 188 p.

167. Giovanni Dotoli, *Le dictionnaire est un discours*, 2022, 152 p.

168. Nicole Coppey, *Lune Soleil de l'Âme*, 2022, 316 p.

169. Michelangelo Dragone, *L'aube de la géométrie divine. L'architecture en France de la fin de l'Empire romain au début du XIIIe siècle*, 2022, sous presse.

170. Michelangelo Dragone, *De Bibracte à Versailles*, 2022, sous presse.

171. Andrei Novac, *à travers prisons et liberté*, illustrations de Flavia Lupu, traduction de Jean-Louis Courriol, préface de Georges Banu, 2022, 148 p.

172. Giovanni Dotoli, *Paris Poésie*, 2022, 376 p.

173. *Négocier sa liberté sous l'ancien régime*, Actes des journées d'étude virtuelles des 22 et 23 juillet 2022 en l'honneur de Rainer Zaiser, sous la direction de Eric Turcat, 2022, 220, 174 p.

174. *Au diapason du poème. Lire la poésie de Giovanni Dotoli*, sous la direction de Maria Leo, Mario Selvaggio et Filomena Villani, 2022, 152 p.

175. Giovanni Dotoli, *Montaigne et Pascal*.

Deux cœurs une âme, 2022, 112 p.

176. Sylvain Josserand, *Retournement / Inversione di rotta*, illustrations de l'Auteur, introduction et traduction en italien par Mario Selvaggio, 2022, 136 p.

177. Alice Machado, *La nostalgie des dieux* / La nostalgia per gli dei, suivi de / seguito da Quelques mots de Kiev… Parole da Kiev, introduction et traduction en italien par Mario Selvaggio, 2022, 152 p.

178. Nicole Coppey, *Le Petit sapin*, dessins de Loredana Cacucciolo, 2022, 32 p.

179. Guillaume Apollinaire, *Le Pont Mirabeau*, édition d'artiste par Giovanni Dotoli, textes par Pierre Brunel, Pierre Caizergues, Sylvestre Clancier, Claude Debon, Giovanni Dotoli, Bernard Franco, Encarnación Medina Arjona, Jean-Pierre Paulhac et Mario Selvaggio, traduction poétique en italien [par] Mario Selvaggio, traduction en chinois [par] Lichao Zhu, traduction en arabe [par] Béchir Ouerhani, mise en musique par Léo Ferré, sonorités par Nicole Coppey, peintures, sculptures, photographies et calligrammes inspirés par le poème [de] Gérard Beaulieu, Jean-Claude Bemben, Michel Bénard, Alain Béral, Nicole Coppey, Michele Damiani, Franceline Debellefontaine, Martine Dinet, Françoise Ducène-Lasvigne, Étienne Fatras, Salvatore Gucciardo, Éliane Hurtado, Paul Kichilov, Hélène Morel, Patrick Navaï, Roland Souchon, Françoise Trémolières, 2023, 124 p. + 16 p. + 68 p.

180. Giovanni Dotoli, *Apollinaire et* Le Pont Mirabeau, 2023, 300 p. + 12 p.

181. Nicole Coppey, *Poèmes de l'attachement & Correspondance poignante entre deux Êtres dans l'Amour*, 2023, 36 p.

182. Giovanni Dotoli, *Change freedom*, translated by Eric Turcat & Hannah Farris, 2023, 128 p.

183. Christophe Boubal, *Dessins*, 2023, 128 p.

184. Claire Inchusta, *Parfums d'alphabets*, 2023, 88 p.

185. Fulvia Fiorino, *Storia di Liliana*, 2023, 136 p.

186. Brice Grudina. *Gli Amori blu*, 2023, 60 p.

187. Giovanni Dotoli, *Épopée*, encres de Michele Damiani, 2023, 92 p.

188. Maribel Peñalver Vicea, *Les titres de film : analyse sémiotico-linguistique*, 2023, 160 p.

189. Giovanni Dotoli, *42 Illuminazioni*, inchiostri di Patrick Navaï, 2023, 80 p.

190. Giovanni Dotoli, *Il pensiero socialista e meridionalista di Tommaso Fiore, Antologia*, 2023, 812 p.

191. *Regalati un'opera d'arte. Catalogo d'asta di opere d'arte di artisti contemporanei*, a cura di Loredana Cacucciolo, Adele Boghetich, Giannatonio Pansini, Francesco Notaro, 2023, 74 p.

192. Giovanni Dotoli, *Défense et illustration de l'art*, 2023, 308 p.

193. Isabelle Chol, *Plasticité et contrainte intérieure. Les Métamorphoses du texte poétique à la fin du XIXe siècle et au début du XXe siècle*, 2023, 320 p.

194. Arthur Thomassin, *Les Éphémères*, 2023, 144 p.

195. Nicole Coppey, *Au Revoir…Rouge… & Correspondance émouvante entre deux Êtres dans l'Amour*, 2023, 36 p.

196. *L'indicible. Déclinaisons du silence, de la censure et de l'autocensure*, sous la direction de María De Los Ángeles Hernández Gómez, 2023, 292 p.

197. *Politique de la ville et aspects linguistiques De la france multiculturelle : Histoire, évolution, contradictions*, sous la direction de Paola Salerni, 2023, 172 p.

198. Sophie Laroque -Texier et Henri Texier, *Paroles fées*, français - italien, 2023, 32 p.

199. Giovanni Dotoli, *Poetic Aphorisms*, Translated by Eric Turcat, 2023, 124 p.